Born to **Die**

BIRTH

↓

LIFE

↓

DEATH

Between birth and death is life.
Live it to the fullest.

Brenda Price

PAGE PUBLISHING, INC.
Conneaut Lake, PA

First originally published by Page Publishing 2020

ISBN 978-1-6624-1817-4 (pbk)
ISBN 978-1-6624-1818-1 (digital)

Printed in the United States of America

DEDICATION

This book is written with heartfelt sympathy to those who have, are currently, or will suffer the effects of bereavement.

IN LOVING MEMORY OF PAT

In loving memory of my oldest niece Pat who passed away on my son's birthday in 2017.

Thank you, Lord, for setting Pat free and providing her a place to abide with Thee.

I still miss Pat; however, I am comforted to know that she no longer has to suffer—that she is in heaven where there is no pain.

As human beings, we, the living, are never emotionally prepared to accept death. It does not matter whether the person dies young or old, from a terminal illness, was tragically killed, dies from natural causes, or is stillborn before having the opportunity to live even one moment in this world. Death is overwhelming and leaves a void that can never be filled. Death comes and steals the presence of someone that we are used to having in this world—our world. It leaves an unthinkable vacancy. We must find ways to appropriately mourn the loss. God has promised to comfort us as we mourn.

> Blessed are those who mourn, because they will be comforted. (Matt. 5:4 Holman Christian Standard Bible)

God has also told us in the Bible that there is a time for everything, including a time to die.

> There is an occasion for everything, and a time for every activity under heaven; a time to give birth and a time to die; (Eccles. 3:1–2 Holman Christian Standard Bible)

I have found journalizing or writing as a means of comfort while dealing with the avalanche of emotions that are brought on by death.

Our culture does not teach us about the destiny of death and how to cope with it or accept it when it comes.

Blessed are those who mourn, because they shall be comforted. (Matt. 5:4 Gideons International New Testament)

Once a person has passed away, no matter how much we wish they were not gone, the reality is they have left this world. We must accept that they have transitioned from this world to the great beyond or wherever you believe they have gone.

Curiously, we tend to speak in a whisper once someone dies as though the deceased can hear us. Or perhaps we believe we will disturb or awaken them. It is a human phenomenon. We may even speak softly out of fear or respect. It just seems to be an unspoken need for silence.

When death comes, most of us will not admit that at that moment in time, we tend to question God. We ask him why the person has died? This is a normal human reaction. That question soon leaves our consciousness, but before it does, we feel guilty for questioning our Maker. We may even entertain the thought that it should have been me (one's self) who died. Yet we know we do not mean it when we say or think it should have been me (one's self) that died.

After the disbelief of the death subsides, the anger sets in. Thoughts of what the deceased will not experience begin to flood our minds.

No marriage, no kids, no graduation, no prom, etc., to name a few. There is a feeling of desperation because the reality is there is nothing we can do to change the fact that the person is dead. The heart no longer beats to pump blood to the rest of the body; the brain no longer thinks to send signals to the rest of the body; the limbs can no longer move, so the skeleton and muscular systems have stopped, the eyes can no longer see; the tongue can no longer taste or speak; the organs can no longer function; and the blood no longer circulates. Essentially, death has come, and all functionality of the body has stopped.

Death may cause your emotions to run the gamut. You may feel some or all the following emotions: disbelief, hopelessness, anger, sorrow, denial, grief, loss, acceptance, and healing.

You will be offered sympathy from others as you grieve. You may hear statements such as "He or she is in a better place," "Don't cry," "Let it go," "Be strong," "You'll be okay," "Your loved one is in a better place," "Your loved one would not want you to grieve," etc. However, this is not true because your loved one would want you to go through the grieving process so you can heal and be whole again. Remember, there is a time for everything. After your loved one or acquaintance passes on, it is not only appropriate to grieve; it is necessary to grieve. If you suppress your grief, it will manifest itself in other ways. You may overeat, drink excessively, display anger verbally or physically, or become emotionally or physically ill, etc.

After a person dies, everything that is done in the present time is for the living. The planning of the funeral, choosing the clothes for the corpse, the flowers for the casket, the writing of the obituary, the decision to cremate or not cremate, and the expressions of sympathy. We may think we are carrying out the final wishes of the deceased, but even if we are, the deceased will never know. So essentially, we are doing everything to please the living.

When my mother passed away in 1973, I felt lost. I could not begin to say how I felt. My ten siblings and I grieved hard. Momma was in the hospital three weeks before her death. The last week prior to her death, she went into a diabetic coma. She also had complications with kidney stones and kidney failure. My momma was only fifty-five at the time of her death. I personally felt she died far too soon.

My husband did not understand my grief. He told me to get over it and stop all the crying. We were unable to reconcile our differences, so we were separated two weeks after my mother's funeral. I was so hurt that my husband could not accept or understand how overwhelmed I was over the loss of my mother. My efforts to get back with my husband were to no avail.

As stated before, death affects everyone differently. What I do know now is you must go through the grieving process before you can begin to heal. There is no specific time frame for grieving. The amount of time of the grieving process will vary from person to person. Just know you must grieve to be whole again after losing someone to death.

Wrapping your brain around and accepting death is a real challenge. Intellectually, you know the person is no longer alive, but in your heart, you still wish that the death was not true. You may find yourself battling between the reality of whether the death is real or a fantasy while secretly hoping that the deceased is still alive. You may almost be in a trance as you go through the motions of planning and/or attending the funeral. As you receive the guests who come to show their sympathy, it is difficult to stay focused. In your heart of hearts, your mind wanders to the deceased, wishing they were there. You could even imagine that the deceased was there. You really do actually appreciate the guests being there. However, because you are overcome by grief, you may not verbalize or display your appreciation. Some of the guests will talk while others will sit silently. Some will bring food and drinks or various other items, including monetary tokens. These acts of concern and kindness and sympathy will make you feel better momentarily, but in the end, you are alone. The aftermath is when you must face the elephant in the room. And that is the fact that the deceased has transitioned from this world to the everlasting, wherever you may believe that is. Now you can face the fact that you will never see, hear, smell, or touch the deceased as a live human being again. The good news is that now you can recall the deceased as often as you like. You have your own private vault of memories. They may make you sad, or you may cry, or you may smile, or your heart may be filled with joy. These are your own private memories, and they are yours to have and to hold. No one can alter them because they belong to you and no one else.

There is light at the end of the tunnel. God will be with you through it all. He will comfort you as no human can. There is a saying that "Time heals." That statement can be true if you are open to the grieving process and that you accept the reality that your loved one or acquaintance has passed away. It is a crucial part of your healing. No matter how you may wish it could be different, the fact is, your loved one or acquaintance is no longer alive. Once you accept this fact and grieve appropriately, the healing can begin. Allow yourself to miss your loved one or acquaintance while you remember the treasured times that you have shared. In all probability, there were happy times, sad times, and many other special times that only you experienced with your loved one or acquaintance. And only you can access the memories of those times at will. Those memories will always be yours and yours alone.

As time passes, moments of sadness will still come, but the frequency will be less. Now you will be able to begin to embrace the joy of having known and having had the opportunity to love the deceased. "Reality is accepting things as they are, not as you wish they were." The reality that all humans share the same commonality, and that is, we are all born to die. At some point, all humans will arrive at the destiny of death.

During the grieving process, God has provided us a remarkable release. That release is tears. The act of crying is cleansing to the soul. Therefore, you should not suppress your tears. Whether you are male or female, boy or girl, man or woman, go ahead and cry. Crying is healthy for the soul. I would recommend that you cry as much and as often as you need to. Cry a river if you need to because crying is an emotional gift from God. You will find and discover after crying, you will feel so much better. While the grieving process is not immediate, crying is a means to help you continue to live through the grieving process. Crying will help to get you to the healing that you need to survive the loss brought on by death. You may be told by others "Do not cry" or "Dry your eyes."

However, you will do yourself an injustice if you do not cry; it will soothe your heavy heart, and it is a "free" gift from God.

Recap of some of the emotions that may be experienced during bereavement as defined in *Webster's II New College Dictionary*.

Disbelief: Reluctance or refusal to believe.
Hopeless: Having no hope, despairing.
Anger: A feeling of great displeasure, hostility, indignation, or exasperation.
Sorrow: Mental anguish or pain caused by injury, loss, or despair.
Denial: A refusal to acknowledge the truth of a statement or allegation.
Grief: Deep mental anguish as over a loss; sorrow.
Loss: An act or process of losing, injury, or suffering caused by losing or being lost.
Acceptance: The act or process of accepting something.
Healing: To restore health or soundness.

The following are a few writings that I wrote during the bereavement of a loved one, acquaintance, or friend. These writings helped me through the grieving process.

Let me reiterate, from our first breath of life, the journey begins on its way to our death. As living human beings, no matter the race, ethnicity, whether rich or poor, young or old, we all share the same commonality, and that is, we are all destined to die. It is not a destination to which we look forward. However, we need to know and accept that, eventually, we will all reach the destination of death.

Remember, between birth and death is life. The longevity of life may vary from a moment to as long as more than a hundred years. I would advise you to live the best life that you can. Live each day to the fullest. Live each day as if it is your last day. Just know, tomorrow is not promised. And at the appointed time, we all shall die. So until death comes, live, because we do not know the day, the time, or place when life here on earth will come to an end. We only know for sure that the time will come when we will all draw our last breath.

MY TIME

"My Time" is a writing about Foster, the nephew of my play daughter, Frann. Foster died eleven days before his seventh birthday. He had an inoperable brain tumor. Foster died far too soon.

My Time

(Written about me, Foster Wyant, by
Brenda Price for my aunt Frann)

My time on earth was short yet sweet.
My family was the best and could never be beat.

I eagerly played and had loads of fun
As I ran, skipped, and enjoyed the warmth of the sun.

I loved you all with a love bigger than the sky.
And my being gone, I am sure, has made you cry.

No reason was given as why I had to go,
Just that my time was over on the earth below.

The essence of my spirit still lingers in your heart
And that's why we will never truly be apart.

I know you have heard me when I whispered in your ear
That's how you have known when I was near.

I transformed from the boy that I used to be
To a heavenly being where I am pain-free.

I can now be found soaring the skies and earth at will.
And though my physical body is not with you, I love you still.

I had my time here on earth with you,
I was born, and day by day, taller I grew.

My body was sick, but I did not complain
Even though my outward appearance was altered
by the incurable issue with my brain.

I was blessed with the ability to do many amazing things,
but I did not take them granted, nor did I feel I was
entitled, just because I was alive.
Instead, I accepted them all and handled them
with extreme care and much pride.

I walked, I talked, I learned at an accelerated speed, I
discerned right from wrong, I swam like a fish, and I
Communicated quite well, all of which
were awesome gifts from God.
As my time to live grew shorter and shorter, I could no longer
do those things, and for you to see me that way, I am
sure was very hard.

Thank you for all the comfort, compassion, and love you gave,
Even for lovingly correcting me when I would misbehave.

I kept the faith until the very end
Because I knew my illness was not a battle for me to win.

I followed God's plan and obeyed His call,
To come to heaven where he has prepared a special place for us all.

Yes, it was my time to leave earth and go to my
eternal home where I have not a care
And I will be waiting for you until it's your time to join me there

DEBORAH ARDREY, THE WOMAN WITH THE MIDAS TOUCH

The writing "Deborah Ardrey, the Woman with the Midas Touch" shared my thoughts of a co-worker who died from a massive stroke. Deborah was active and appeared to be very healthy. Her death affected me intensely. It was hard to believe she was gone. I missed her at work, and I missed her friendship.

Deborah Ardrey, the Woman with the Midas Touch

Did you know Deborah Ardrey, the woman with the
Midas Touch who was always meticulously dressed?
The woman who always in all things did her best.

In all facets of her life, she lived to the utmost,
But never about her many accomplishments did she boast.

She believed in the best quality of life and always wanted all to be well.
Therefore, on the negative, she was not one to dwell.

To her husband, she was a devoted wife.
She was an outstanding mother to the two children to whom she gave life.

Deborah was a hard worker, toiling from morning until late in the night,
Making ready so that things for tomorrow would be right.

Deborah was an organizer for her whole family,
Making sure every function was together to the "tee."

She was a grandmother, who was as proud as could be
Because Jaton was the greatest grandson ever in her eyes, you see.

Her four sisters were more important and precious than
words can say,
Because she was the youngest, so she looked to them
to show her the way.

Not a day went by without Deborah speaking of Robert
with whom she shared and cared and fulfilled many a
dream.
Together, the two of them, they were quite a team.

Deborah dearly loved and adored LaChrisha and
Gregory as they were the apple of her eye.
And they realized and appreciated this close family tie.
She guided them and did not take any stuff.
She taught them, and they know sometimes love has to be tough.

Deborah cared about her friends, whether young or old.
She became a mentor and role model for so many, the
number is untold.

Deborah greeted you warmly with her friendly smile.
She was a woman who always went the extra mile.
Once you met Deborah, there was a special tie
Because she was a woman on whom you could surely
Rely.

When she talked in her expressive way,
Others would stop and take a listen to what she had to
say.

Deborah understood the importance of her roots.
She held in high esteem her ancestors, but she did not try
To fill their boots.

The lessons from the yesteryears made her life better than
theirs.
So she shared what she knew to help others manage
difficult cares.

She had a style of her own with which none can compare,
And you must agree she was, indeed, rare.

Tan, the president/CEO at her job, insightfully shared
Remember the good times with Deborah, to show her that
you cared.
He said, "Pray. Do it now. Do it every day, Do it today."

And be comforted to know with the passage of time, the
Pain of this great loss will go away.

Deborah was concerned in her last days about her own
Mother's fate,
But to see the outcome, she was unable to wait.

Though we all wanted her to stay, she had to go
Because her home was no longer here on earth below.

Having known Deborah Ardrey, the woman with the
Midas Touch, as we did, we surely will understand why by
and by
She had to exit to her home in the sky.

Dressed in her best outfit of all with her angel wings
She soared through the galaxy and all those outer space
Things.

She reached her destination, which is heaven above.
Now she is at peace, basking in that eternal love.

Lovingly written in memory of Deborah Ardrey by Brenda Price
January 23, 2000

GABRIELLE, THE ANGEL WHO CAME TO EARTH

The writing "Gabrielle, the Angel Who Came to Earth" is about a baby who lived less than twelve months. She was an angel who came to earth, who soon returned to heaven. She was my friend Patricia's friend's daughter.

Gabrielle, the Angel Who Came to Earth

My name is Gabrielle, the name you gave me at the time of my birth,
My home has been about seven months with you while I was here on earth.
Even though my life on earth was short, all is well.
And this is the story that I now want to tell,
God gave me the chance to come to earth for a little while,
He wanted me to make you happy and make you smile,
He wanted me to let you see
How sweet and gentle an angel can be.
He wanted me to bless you with love,
The kind that can only come from heaven above.
He wanted me to leave with you a memory with which none can compare,
And that is why I came to earth with you, myself, to share.
He wanted me to let you know that I am okay
And that His Word He now wants you to obey.
He wants you to fret not and let not your heart be troubled
Because of having me, your blessings will be doubled.
Yes, I am Gabrielle, the angel who came to earth, it is true,
And though I am no longer here, I don't want you to be blue.
Because I have returned home,
But I am not alone, I am with Jesus, who is on His throne.

Mommy and Daddy, I want you to believe in angels too.
So that you will know, I will always be there with you!

Lovingly,
Gabrielle, "your angel"

As told by Brenda Price, on my behalf
January 11, 2000

MY JACKIE

The writing "My Jackie" depicts my thoughts of Jackie, a homeless woman whom I met while volunteering at a thrift store. The thrift store was called Great Things and was owned by my church, Friendship Missionary Baptist Church in Charlotte, North Carolina.

Jackie came to the store frequently for clean clothes. Ms. Rachel, who ran the store, made sure we held back clothes for Jackie. Almost daily, Jackie would come into the store to get the clothes that had been saved for her. Soon after that, Jackie would be strutting up and down Beatties Ford Road in her new outfits. One day, she changed three times.

I quickly became attached to Jackie. I looked forward to her visits and our conversations.

One night, I was watching the local news, and I heard that a pedestrian named Jackie had been killed while crossing Beatties Ford Road. My heart began to pound. I said to myself, *I wonder if it is "my Jackie?"* In my heart, I knew it was her, but I needed confirmation. The store was closed, so I could not call there. I called the Long & Son Mortuary Service, which was just up the street from the thrift store. I asked whether the Jackie who had been killed was the homeless woman who often walked up and down Beatties Ford Road. The answer, which I had anticipated, was yes. My heart was broken when my fear was confirmed. I wrote the poem "My Jackie" in honor and remembrance of my homeless friend, Jackie.

In Loving Memory of
Jacqueline Henley

9/23/62 – 6/5/09
Always in our Hearts

My Jackie

My Jackie, I cannot believe you are gone.
No longer the streets of this earth do you have to roam.
No more do you have to eat the leftovers of others from the trash
Because God sent a band of angels to rescue you from that car crash.
No more do you have to seek a place to sleep
Because your soul is now with God to keep.
No more do you have to find socks, shoes,
and clothes to wear because in this
world no longer do you have a care.
No more worry about whether the temperature
is too cold or too hot or trying
to find that special drink that would hit the spot.
No longer do you need to struggle just to live
your way because God Almighty
has had the last say.
He said to you, my Jackie, it is time for you
to come to your heavenly place,
where for eternity you now have your very own space.
Never again will it be boarded up to keep you out,
Now you can run around and sing and shout.

It is a mansion, layered with rubies and gold.
You have robes and crowns and
an abundance of everything untold.
For your feet that used to ache, they have
been renewed, make no mistake
You can float about the heavens as much as you like.
No more worry about time because you will never lose track.
The world will miss you very much
Because, my Jackie, so many lives did you touch.
You said to one friend, "You love me, don't
you?" She answered, "Of course, I do,
and God loves you too."
Your friend told you to smile as you faced
troubles of your world, and you would grin
with the innocence of a little girl.
Oh, my Jackie, I will miss you as I shed a tear,
But with highest reverence to God, I give the
Greatest cheer because, my Jackie, you
have reached your ultimate goal
Because with God you have rested your soul.

LOUIS MOBLEY

I wrote the writing "Louis Mobley" who was my mother's brother and my uncle. He was the youngest of twelve children. He was truly a unique individual.

He Gave His Best and Now He Is at Rest

After giving to this world his very best,
God called Louie home to eternal rest.
In his unique way, he lived his life,
And without complaint, he endured his strife.
And in the end, he entered into a peaceful sleep
And gave to Jesus his soul to keep.
From the world, he went away
To God's kingdom, there to stay.
No more pain does he have to bear
Because God has rescued him from his every care.
His spirit now dwells in the Promised Land
As revealed in God's divine plan.
Yes, we, the living, know he gave his best.
Praise God, praise God, he is now at rest.

Brenda Price
"Rosebud"

STILLBORN

My first grandson was stillborn. I wrote about his birth/death in memory of the precious moments I shared with him.

Stillborn

My first grandson, Johnny Price Johnson, was stillborn. He was perfectly formed. A mere thirteen and a half inches long with ten tiny fingers and ten tiny toes; unfortunately, the umbilical cord got wrapped around his neck in the womb. He was dead several days before his delivery. His mother noticed the baby inside her was no longer moving. She called the doctor and made an appointment to see him in his office. The doctor informed the mother and my son that the baby was dead after completing the examination. The mother was hospitalized. Labor was induced. The mother had to go through hours of labor even though she knew the baby would be born dead.

The mother and my son held their son for hours after his birth. I traveled from Lithonia, Georgia, to Huntington, West Virginia, in support of the parents. I held the little hands of my stillborn grandson. He was beautiful and so small. A tiny little angel. It was sad yet a joy. Sad that Johnny Price (the name my son gave his son after my father) would not have the chance to grow up and be loved by his earthly family. Yet what a joy to know he had returned to heaven to be with God—the God who gives life, the God who takes life away. It was a joy to know that my firstborn grandson was now an angel. He was so precious to see as sweet as can be. Tiny little face, never intended to be a part of the living human race. God swept him away, so in heaven with him he could stay.

Tragedy

Death brings emotional devastation no matter when it comes. However, a tragic death is even more devastating. That is particularly because it is a surprise. No advance notice. No illness, just sudden death, caused by an unseen tragedy.

My family had to endure two tragic deaths in 1983 within two weeks of each other. First, my great-niece, Monique, died in a house fire. She was four years old. She died toward the end of May. She would have been five years old on August 24 that year. My beautiful little niece was so young, so sweet, and so innocent at the time of her death. She had so much potential that would never be realized. Monique's death was a tremendous loss to her mother, Linda, and her sister, Wanda. We will never know the pain that gripped their hearts.

Second, my twenty-seven-year-old nephew, Marvin, died after lifting the tarp covering the house of a friend that was being fumigated. He died immediately from a heart attack from being exposed to the fumes from the chemicals used for the fumigation. Had Marvin known the danger, he would not have lifted the tarp. These two deaths were both tragic. The tragedy of it all was hard on my entire family.

My sister Fannie and her husband, Melvin, were Marvin's parents. They grieved hard and long over my nephew's death. He was their only child. I still miss my nephew, Marvin. He was my confidant. I shared everything with him. He was a great dancer. He tried to teach me to dance.

It did not work because I still cannot dance.

SHARLENE DOMINIQUE BROWN

Sharlene Dominique Brown, my beautiful niece, died from stab wounds fifteen days before her twenty-first birthday. Her death was another heartbreaking tragedy. It rocked the consciousness of the small country town of Chester, South Carolina.

The following poem was written with love about my niece, Sharlene.

In Tribute to Sharlene

Home to a Better Place

She fought the fight of today's youth,
Living and loving and searching for truth.
Innocent of the dangers that were around that
would eventually claim her life.
Amid the laughter, bearing a son, the fun, and the
strife. And even though we will no longer see her
beautiful face, we know she went home to a better
place. We will always have the memory of her
short earthly existence in our heart, which from us
will never depart.
Sharlene, we love you and will miss you dearly, but
we who are left to mourn can see clearly that you
did your very best, and now God has given you your rest.
Sharlene, God heard your cry for *help* when
others just stood by. He sent angels with swiftness
to bring you your wings, so to *heaven* you could fly.
So you no longer have to search for the best of anything
because you are home in a better place
with the *King*.

Lovingly,
The Family
Inspired by your mother, Pat

THE LAST MILE

The "Last Mile" was written for a co-worker whose grandmother had passed away.

The Last Mile

The last mile I had to go alone
To finish the journey to my heavenly home.
You were there to care for me as much as you could,
But God said come, and I obeyed, as I should.
He said, "Well done, your earthly tasks are complete.
Not one more tomorrow on earth shall you repeat.
You have labored hard, it's time to take your rest.
Now lay your head upon my breast.
The breath I gave you, I must now take away.
Angels will comfort those you leave behind day by day."
I went to the end of the tunnel to that bright light.
There I saw the most magnificent sight
The heavenly host gathered to open the gate,
And I moved swiftly so I would not be late.
My heart stopped beating, and to my surprise,
I leaped into eternity and heard the cries.
They were sounds of joy that I made it in
To be with Jesus, man's best friend.
No more pain do I have to bear,
As I have gone to glory, I do declare.
Cry, as you shall for a little while
But know, alone I had to go the last mile.

In loving memory of Arlivia Early
To Shelitha Mills and family
With heartfelt sympathy from Brenda Price
February 3, 2000

MY LAST TEAR

The writing "My Last Tear" was written to honor Sharon Holley. She was a beautiful young professional woman who died too soon. Sharon was gentle yet strong. She was renowned for being an exemplary children's dentist, as well as a role model to many. Sharon was always sharing with family, friends, and strangers. She had a caring spirit, always looking out for her fellowman.

My Last Tear

My last tear that I cried was for you because in my mind's
eye, I knew you would be blue after my last breath
I would take. I knew your heart would break.

After I died, I came home to the celestial skies here
where all the awesomeness of God abides.

So live on, my mother, Georgianna, live on my brother,
Jerome, and all the rest of my family, which is too numerous
to name, yet your importance to me was just the same.

Accept that I had to go before you because my end had
come, as only God knew. I wanted to stay, but God
had the final say. So he called my number, and I had to
obey that final call. My body was tired after all.

The pain had become too much to endure, and I had grown too
weak to go on, and my physical decline you witnessed I am sure.

All my earthly duties were complete, so God said,
"Come to me and take your heavenly seat."

Remember my legacy... I loved, I cared, I shared and I
lived outside the box, always going beyond the "norm"
to do my very best, knowing all the time, when I fell
short of my goal that God would do the rest.

During my lifetime, I experienced and accomplished much
that's because God blessed me with that special touch.

Keep the faith, and in God, put your trust. Just know he will comfort you as you mourn, and just know, mourn you must.

Yes, I have shed my last tear for you. Now as the tears fall from your eyes for me, don't cry too long because, you see, when your number is called, we shall meet again in the great beyond.

Lovingly penned by Miss Brenda for Sharon

IN LOVING MEMORY OF PAT

In loving memory of my oldest niece Pat who passed away on my son's birthday in 2017.

The following was written in memory of the first anniversary of Pat's death. Writing about Pat helped me through the grieving process. It was written expressly for her sisters Linda, Bernice, Julie, Teresa, and Gloria, also for her children, Karen and Carl, as well as her grandsons, Stephon, CJ, and Terio. I also shared the writing with my family and friends too so that a glimpse of Pat would stay fresh in their memory.

I still miss Pat; however, I am comforted to know that she no longer has to suffer—that she is in heaven where there is no pain.

Remembering Pat

Patricia Ann Coleman Brown
(Affectionately called "Pat")

Sunrise: January 3, 1954
Sunset: September 7, 2017

Pat was unique, never finding it necessary to be like others. She was independent with a style of her own (never wanting to be a burden to anyone).

Pat did not like fanfare. She preferred a life without drama though she endured her share of drama during her lifetime. She did not seek out the drama it found its way to her.

Pat bore her cross without complaint. She lasted until the end without becoming faint.

Pat was kindhearted and did not hesitate in her giving.

She crocheted hats and scarves and other things, and she made jellies, jams, and preserves to share while she was living.

Pat greeted everyone with warmness. She often used the phrase "How you doing, darling?" When she met someone new, she would say, "My name is Patricia, but they call me Pat."

Pat loved to watch movies. She collected and
listened to radios. She read many books and was
one of the best cooks. She was a great dancer, and
she exercised often to stay trim back in the day.

Pat was a caregiver. She often sat with and cared
for the sick and shut-in.

Pat loved her family and friends. She especially loved her children, Karen, Carl, Sharlene (deceased), Stephon, CJ, and Terio. Her love for them was from the very depth of her heart. With them and others, her vast knowledge she did gladly impart.

Pat loved flowers. Her favorite was sunflowers. She grew them along with peppers, tomatoes, okra, squash, and greens on a yearly basis.

Pat started calling Momma, "Momma Lessie," when she was a young girl. It caught on, and that is what our family called Momma from then on.

Pat did not have much; however, she did not live beyond her means. She enjoyed shopping at thrift stores where she found many treasures, especially yarn, purses, and books. She went to the store several times a week. Before her walking became challenged, she would walk to the store, post office, and Laundromat. Pat often gave small gifts, such as candy, cards, candles, bananas, or a special drink, like POM, or at Christmastime, a noncolored Pepsi. Pat's unselfishness will always be remembered. It was not the size of her gifts that mattered; it was her caring touch.

Pat was a surrogate mother at a very young age to her four younger sisters at the time. She cared for them; she protected them and kept them on the straight and narrow when her mother was unavailable to do so.

Pat served at her church at special programs or banquets. She gave as much money as she could, when she could, especially at our home church, Old Wilson Baptist Church. She wanted to be sure she had a space for her burial when the time came. Pat cooked great desserts, including egg custards to share, letting others know about them that she did care.

Pat believed in and put her faith and trust in God. She ended her letters and cards with "Keep the Faith, Pat."

Pat raised her grandson, Stephon, from age four, after the untimely death of his mother, Sharlene. She gave Stephon the best that she had to give so that a better life he would have the opportunity to live.

Pat was proud of her daughter, Karen, who has accomplished so much thus far in life. Most of all, Pat appreciated Karen's help in raising Stephon and for taking care of her during her battle with cancer. In Pat's words, "I am so thankful that Karen takes the time to fool with me."

Shortly before Pat died, she walked to the altar, though she could barely walk or stand, to pray for her family, especially for her buddy, Linda. She knew her time on earth was drawing nigh, and she wanted to be sure she would see her family in the afterlife. She wanted to be sure her family knew and had accepted Jesus as their Savior to ensure their salvation. Pat loved and cared for all of us, even in her dying days.

Pat was ready to go home to heaven. She was excited about seeing Momma Lessie and Granddaddy again.

God answered Pat's prayers by allowing her to stay in her right mind and by not letting her suffer too long. He replied to the desire of her heart by taking her to heaven where saints belong.

Pat had done all she was assigned to do here on earth. Now she is basking in her new birth—born again into eternal life where it is calm and free of strife.

Pat kept the faith and made it in (away from this world being engulfed by destruction and sin).

Thank you, Lord, for setting Pat free
and providing her a place
to abide with Thee.

Until we meet again…

Aunt Brenda

Bottom line, God has the last word when it is our time to die. When we are born, he gives us free will. As we mature, we learn that we have to make a decision about and for our eternity. We can decide to go to hell or accept Jesus as our Savior, be forgiven for our sins, and spend eternity in heaven after our death. There, we will have no more cares at all; no ups, no downs, no pains, no tears, no fears, no disappointments, no heartaches, no heartbreaks, and no deaths. Find comfort in knowing after we die (our spirit and our soul), we will go to heaven to be with God.

> Therefore, though we are always confident and know that while we are at home in the body we are away from the Lord, for we walk by faith, not by sight yet we are confident and satisfied to be out of the body and at home with the Lord. (2 Cor. 5:6–8 Holman Christian Standard Bible)

Therefore, we should not fret about death because Jesus has promised

> In my Father's house are many dwelling places; if not, I would have told you. I am going away to prepare a place for you. If I go away and prepare a place for you, I will come back and receive you to myself so that where I am you may be also. (John 14:2–3 Holman Christian Standard Bible)

Remember, between birth and death is life.
Live it to the fullest.

ABOUT THE AUTHOR

Brenda Price was born in August 1944 in Rural Chester County in South Carolina. She was raised on the family farm in Chester, South Carolina. She is the fifth child of eleven children.

Brenda is seventy-six years of age. She is blessed to have lived this long since her mother died at fifty-five, and her father died at sixty-four.

Brenda recalls her childhood years working on the farm, picking cotton and diligently performing other tasks to keep the farm going, along with her siblings. The first six weeks of school were spent harvesting the farm, which meant she only went to school when it rained during that period.

After graduating from high school (Finley High School class of 1962), Brenda moved to Harrisburg, Pennsylvania, to live with her sister Fannie and her family. This was to ensure she would have a better opportunity to find lucrative employment. She was hired by Bell of Pennsylvania. She worked in the telecommunications industry for thirty-seven years.

Brenda is the proud and devoted mother of one son, Bruce, who is a highly intelligent and well educated black man, and the loving and caring grandmother of a beautiful granddaughter, Brianna, and handsome grandson, Anil. Her first grandson, Johnny, was stillborn.

Brenda took the advice of her niece, Linda, who thought a book needed to be written about the process of dealing with grief brought on by death. After the death of her oldest niece, Patricia (Pat), who died in 2017, Brenda became even more determined than ever to write and get published the book *Born to Die*. Writing this book helped Brenda grieve and accept Pat's death.

This book is for all humanity. Some of the writings date back many years. However, God gave Brenda the words and ability to compile this book in its entirety. Prayerfully, it will bring some light during a time of darkness brought on by death.

God gave Brenda this book, and because she is a giving individual, she is now giving you, all the world, a chance to benefit from God's gift to her.

To God be the glory!

CPSIA information can be obtained
at www.ICGtesting.com
Printed in the USA
BVHW071225220221
600770BV00005B/458

9 781662 418174